One World

In the City

Valerie Guin

FRANKLIN WATTS
LONDON•SYDNEY

Note
about the series
One World is designed to encourage young readers to find out more about people and places in the wider world. The photographs have been carefully selected to stimulate discussion and comparison.

First published in 2007 by Franklin Watts
338 Euston Rd, London NW1 3BH

Franklin Watts Australia
Hachette Children's Books
Level 17/207 Kent St, Sydney, NSW 2000

© Franklin Watts 2007

Editor: Caryn Jenner
Designer: Louise Best
Art director: Jonathan Hair
Map: Ian Thompson
Reading consultant: Hilary Minns, Institute of Education, Warwick University

Acknowledgements: Toby Adamson/Still Pictures: 14. P Birchalls/Eye Ubiquitous: 3, 16. Dean Conger/Corbis: 21. R Craven/Eye Ubiquitous: endpapers, 27. David Cummings/Eye Ubiquitous: 22. James Davis Worldwide: 15t. Markus Dlouhy/Still Pictures: 8. Mark Edwards/Still Pictures: 12. Macduff Everton/Corbis: 9. Peter Frismuth/Still Pictures: 6. Dylan Garcia/Still Pictures: 15b. Maurice Harvey/ Hutchison: 23. Jeremy Horner/ Hutchison: 18. Jan Butchofsky-Houser/Corbis: 10. Hympendahl/Still Pictures: 25. Graham Kitching/Ecoscene: cover, 26. Frank Leather/Eye Ubiquitous: 24. James Marshall/Corbis: 20. Bilie Rafaeli/Hutchison: 11. Stephen Rafferty/Eye Ubiquitous: 7. Mike Reed/Eye Ubqiuitous: 13. Liba Taylor/Hutchison: 19. Paul Thompson/Eye Ubiquitous: 17.

A CIP catalogue record for this book is available from the British Library

ISBN 9780749676582

Dewey Classification: 307.76

Printed in Malaysia

Franklin Watts is a division of Hachette Children's Books.

Contents

City life

All around the world, there are cities. A city is a large town where many people live and work.

This is a **map** of all the **countries** in the world. Read this book to find out about cities in countries all over the world.

▶ These children are walking along a city street. In this book, you will see lots of different things in many different cities.

Old and new

Some cities are very old. The city of Rome in Italy is more than 2,000 years old. Even though there are now many **modern** buildings in Rome, you can still see the remains of the old city.

In the past few years, many people have moved to the city of Shenzhen in China. Workers have built many new buildings for people to live and work in.

Busy streets

Many cities have lots of shops and houses close together, so it is easy for people to walk from place to place. This busy street is in the city of Quito in Ecuador.

People in the city of Los Angeles in the United States usually drive their cars to get about. Busy roads called freeways link the different places in the city.

Buildings

People in cities need homes, shops, schools, offices, hospitals and many other buildings. In Mexico City, the buildings are spread over about 2,000 **square kilometres** of land.

Singapore is on an island of only about 600 square kilometres, so space is limited. Tall buildings called **skyscrapers** stretch up towards the sky. Building up high saves space in cities.

Getting about

Many people take buses to get about on the streets of the city. This is the bus **station** in the city of Accra in Ghana.

Part of the city of Hong Kong, China, is on an island. The Star Ferry takes people between the island and the mainland.

Underground trains travel below some city streets. This one is in London, Britain, where underground trains were first invented.

Places to visit

There are many interesting places to visit in cities. The Eiffel Tower is a famous sight in the city of Paris, France. From the top of the tower, there are beautiful views of Paris.

This is the famous Opera House
in Sydney, Australia. It was
built to look like a sailing ship.
Inside the building are **theatres**
where people can watch a play
or hear a concert.

Shopping

In cities, you can buy many things at shops and **markets**. This market is called a souk. It is in the city of Marrakech in Morocco.

At this floating market in Bangkok, Thailand, people buy and sell **goods** from boats. Instead of using money, they often exchange one thing for another.

Jobs in the city

▶ There are many different jobs to do in the city. This police officer is directing **traffic** on a busy street in Lagos, Nigeria.

Taxi drivers take people
wherever they want to go
in the city. This woman is
a taxi driver in the city of
Irkutsk in Russia.

Fun in the city

Most cities have parks where
people can have fun outdoors.
Many people play cricket in this
park in the city of Calcutta, India.

The city of Rio de Janeiro in Brazil has a long sandy beach next to the Atlantic Ocean. The warm weather means that people in the city can have fun playing in the sea.

Special events

People in cities often have street parades to celebrate holidays and festivals. This float is part of a parade in Kyoto, Japan.

These marathon runners race through the streets of Düsseldorf in Germany. Marathons are held in many cities to raise money for charity. People come to watch and cheer the runners.

City lights

Many cities are still busy at
night. This is New York City in
the United States. It is called
"the city that never sleeps"!

At night, the lights of Liverpool in Britain are reflected in the water of the River Mersey.

All around the world

There are cities all around the world.

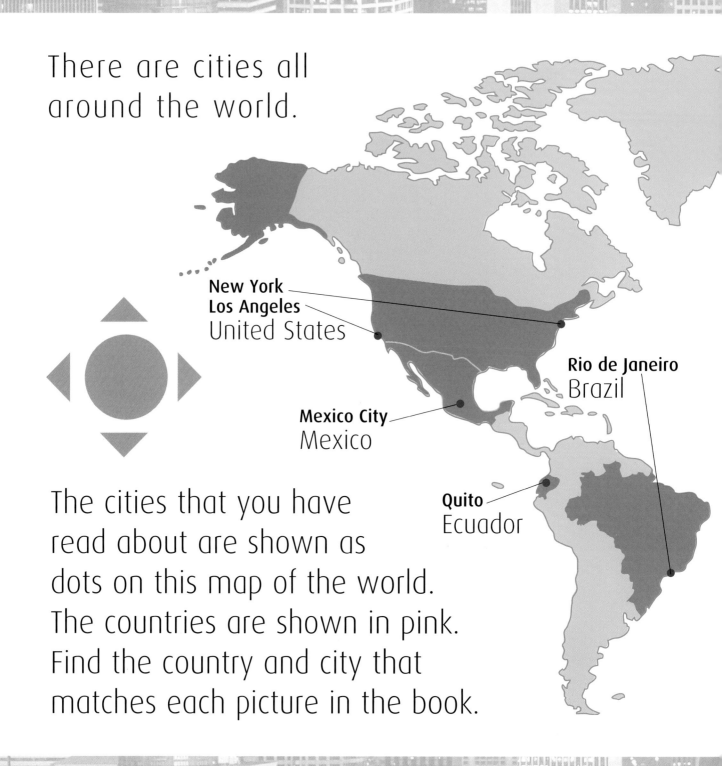

New York
Los Angeles
United States

Rio de Janeiro
Brazil

Mexico City
Mexico

Quito
Ecuador

The cities that you have read about are shown as dots on this map of the world. The countries are shown in pink. Find the country and city that matches each picture in the book.

Liverpool
London
Britain

Düsseldorf
Germany

Irkutsk
Russia

Paris
France

Kyoto
Japan

Shenzhen
Hong Kong
China

Rome
Italy

Bangkok
Thailand

Calcutta
India

Accra
Ghana

Lagos
Nigeria

Singapore City
Singapore

Marrakech
Morocco

Sydney
Australia

Glossary

countries   places with their own governments

goods   things that are bought and sold

map   a drawing that shows where places are

market   a place where people buy and sell things

modern   new

skyscrapers   very tall buildings

square kilometres   a measurement of an area of land

station   a place where people get on and off buses or trains

theatre   a building where people see a play or concert

traffic   the cars and trucks that are on a road

Index